www.ChristedBride.com

TAKEN FROM THE BOOK:

Resurrection Journey OF THE *Christed Bride*

As an "Inner Deep Work" Invitation

As learned from *SonShineRose*
Passed on to You...

You Are
the Beloved of Father and Mother God
and From the Kingdom of Light

MY RESURRECTION JOURNEY

A Workbook Invitation

By MarieLucinda Anderson

Copyright © 2020 Christed Bride dot com LLC
Original Printing, 2020
All rights reserved, including all text and written materials, images, illustrations and drawings.

ISBN: 978-1-7355885-1-3
For more information, please contact:
Publisher: **Christed Bride dot com LLC**
8825 N. 23rd Avenue, Suite 100 • Phoenix, Arizona 85201
info@ChristedBride.com • **www.ChristedBride.com**

Cover Design by MarieLucinda Anderson

~ WARNING ~

No portion of this book is to be copied or reproduced in writing, as illustrations, or in sound recordings without prior written permission. Any unauthorized copying, reproduction, and distribution through any optical system, written and sound productions, and voice recordings based on this material is strictly prohibited. Any copy made of one or more images and or text, placed on the internet or any other media, printed, video or otherwise will be considered an infringement of copyright and is subject to criminal or civil prosecution as provided by law.

PRINTED IN THE USA

...And if the Spirit of the One who raised Yahushua (Jesus) from the dead is living in You, then the One who raised the Messiah Yahushua from the dead will also give life to Your mortal bodies through His Spirit living in You.

~ Romans 8:11 Complete Jewish Bible (CJB)

Purification Fire

Therefore, my dear friends, since we have these promises, let us Purify ourselves from everything that can defile either Body or Spirit, and strive to be completely Holy, out of reverence for God.

2 Corinthians 7:1 Complete Jewish Bible (CJB)

Dedication

"This **Workbook** has been dedicated to YOU, the Family of Light here upon this Earth plane. As you travel through third dimensional Lessons of Light and Dark, may the Father and Mother of Heaven Light up Your path and also Light You up from the inside out!!!!"

"Come along... **Come take this journey and follow Yahushua (Jesus)**...and be transformed from one degree of Glory to another degree of Glory to another degree of Glory until You are changed into His Image above."

I Love you my Family of Light... I AM Forever yours,

SonShine Rose

2 Corinthians 3:18

Complete Jewish Bible (CJB) Version
So all of us, with faces unveiled, see as in a mirror the Glory of the Lord; and we are being changed into his very image, from one degree of Glory to the next, by Adonai the Spirit.

Amplified Version
And all of us, as with unveiled face, [because we] continued to behold [in the Word of God] as in a mirror the Glory of the Lord, are constantly being transfigured into His very own image in ever-increasing splendor and from one degree of Glory to another; [for this comes] from the Lord [Who is] the Spirit.

The Message Version
Whenever, though, they turn to face God as Moses did, God removes the veil and there they are—face-to-face! They suddenly recognize that God is a living, personal presence, not a piece of chiseled stone. And when God is personally present, a living Spirit, that old, constricting legislation is recognized as obsolete. We're free of it! All of us! Nothing between us and God, our faces shining with the brightness of his face. And so we are transfigured much like the Messiah, our lives gradually becoming brighter and more beautiful as God enters our lives and we become like Him.

Complete Orthodox Bible Version
NOW all of us, with unveiled faces, seeing the kavod of Adoneinu [SHEMOT 16:7; 24:17] as if reflected in a mirror, are being transformed into the same demut from kavod to kavod, even as from HaAdon HaRuach.

The Voice Version
NOW all of us, with our faces unveiled, reflect the Glory of the Lord as if we are mirrors; and so we are being transformed, metamorphosed, into His same image from one radiance of Glory to another, just as the Spirit of the Lord accomplishes it.

Table of Contents

Purification Fire	1-2
Dedication	3-4
Blank spacer page	5
Table of Contents	6-7
Blank spacer page	8
Your Invitation	9-10
Blank spacer page	11
Angel Power	12
I Choose to Dream	13-14
My Transmutation Journey from Darkness back into the Light	15-16
The Blessing of Returning Back to God	17-18
Taking off Your Duality Masks	19-20
Open Your Sacred Soul Scrolls	21
The Mitzvah for Crossing Over	22
Time to Remove my Duality Masks	23-24
Assessing Your Direction	25-26
SECTION 1 ~ Ready	**27-28**
Abandonment ~ Never Alone	29-30
Betrayal ~ Faithfulness	31-32
Resentment ~ Pleasure	33-34
Judgment ~ Forgiveness	35-36
Envy ~ Friendliness	37-38
Surprise ~ Engagement	39-40
Cruelty ~ Kindness	41-42
Greed ~ Giving	43-44
Grief ~ Joy	45-46
Pity ~ Compassion	47-48
Isolation ~ Public	49-50
Shame ~ Confidence	51-52
Indignation ~ Respect	53-54
SECTION 2 ~ Let's Do This	**55-56**
Sadness ~ Hopefulness	57-58
Enmity ~ Friendship	59-60
Lonely ~ Loved	61-62
Bewitched ~ Let go	63-64
Defiance ~ Peace	65-66
Loathing ~ Approval	67-68
Rage ~ Harmony	69-70
Pain ~ Assistance	71-72
Vexed ~ Quietness	73-74
Anger ~ Gentleness	75-76
Torment ~ Contentment	77-78
Hatred ~ Admiration	79-80
Fear ~ Courage	81-82
Pride ~ Humility	83-84
Bitterness ~ Sweetness	85-86
SECTION 3 ~ Last Push	**87-88**
Lust ~ Divine Love	89-90
Contempt ~ Honor	91-92
Disobedience ~ Surrender	93-94
Disgust ~ Liking	95-96
Disenchanted ~ Encouraged	97-98
Separation ~ Union	99-100
Doubt ~ Trust	101-102
Remorse ~ Happiness	103-104

Table of Contents

SECTION 3 ~ Last Push Continued
   Disapproval ~ Endorsed...105-106
   Distrust ~ Optimism..107-108
   Despair ~ Hope...109-110
   Guilt ~ Cleansed..111-112
Finished and Proud of You..**113-114**
The Pivotal Question..**115-116**
   Two Choices...117-118
The Awakening...**119-120**
ISIS Temple Inscription..**121-122**
Hear Me, O Son's of Light...**123**
   Co-Creating Begins with You...124
   As Above so Below quote by Hermes Trismegistus..125
   Essene Communion Introduced..126
   The Decision...127-128
   Parting the Veils with 7 Hermetic Principles..129-130
   Living Sacrifice...131-132
     Blank spacer page 133
Ascension...**134**
   The Invitation...135-136
     Blank spacer page 137
Glorified Body Restoring...**138**
   Cocooned...139-140
   Born Again...141-142
   Fountain of Living Water...143-144
   Time to Turn Our Lights On..145
SonShine Rose Autograph Page...146

❖❖❖

TO ORDER: Book-Workbook-Angel Communion~Audio/Visual Book........................147-148
Audio/Visual Book Preview..149
For Further Personal Studies..150
Deeper Inner Work Section..151
  Worksheet: Trauma Reconciliation..152-153
  Worksheet: Shifting Beliefs and Judgments...154-155
Photography Credits and Other Image Credits...156-157
Model Credits...158
Christed Bride Logo..159
Please Meet the Author..**160**
Notes...161-163

ALL SCRIPTURE QUOTES
www.Biblegateway.com **Complete Jewish Bible (CJB)** Translation
Copyright © 1998 by David H. Stern. All rights reserved.

ESSENE SCRIPTURES FOR COMMUNIONS
The ESSENE GOSPEL OF PEACE **(Book One/Two/Three/Four)** The Original Hebrew and Aramaic Texts
Translated and edited by EDMOND BORDEAUX SZEKELY - MCMLXXXI
INTERNATIONAL BIOGENIC SOCIETY - Book Design by Golondrina Graphics
Copyright @ 1981, by the International Biogenic Society
Printed In the United States of America-All Rights Reserved

www.ChristedBride.com

This is *Your* Invitation

to open up your HEART really big
and allow the release of
all trauma and past karmic debts...
to be lifted and released from your life
NOW and Forever More.

To FIRST experience the deep cleaning of
your DNA from Today...
all the way back through your ancestral history...
deep through every incarnation of
YOUR Earth School's experiences...

Spread open your Heart Chakra and
Take a Deep Cleansing Breath

And Let's Begin...

I,_____
(Write your Full Birth Name)

— I CHOOSE TO DREAM —

A New Dream of Love...

Possible

Eternal Life Here
&
NOW

Dated:_____

Welcome

to My New Dream...

MY TRANSMUTATION JOURNEY

from

DARKNESS

back into

Returning back to God's Blessings:
Place your Drawing or Photo Here

The Blessing of Returning to God

*When the time arrives that all these things
have come upon you,
both the blessing and the curse which
I have presented to you;
and you are there among the nations to which
ADONAI your God has driven you; then, at last,
you will start thinking about
what has happened to you;
² and you will return to
ADONAI your God and pay attention
to what he has said,
which will be exactly what I am ordering
you to do today — you and your children,
with all your heart and all your being.
³ At that point,
ADONAI your God will reverse your exile
and show you mercy;
he will return and gather you from all the peoples
to which ADONAI your God scattered you.*

~ Deuteronomy 30:1-3 • Complete Jewish Bible (CJB)

Taking Off Your Duality Masks

First... You must be willing to STOP...

Look deep into your **Masks of Darkness**...
Love those aspects and emotional pieces...
Turn the Lights on and see the other side...
Then join them together in Perfect Holiness and Union.

Shall we Begin?

Let us NOW

Open **YOUR** Sacred Soul **SCROLLS**...

And Peek into The Duality Lessons

that **YOU have**

learned

here in Earth School...

The Mitzvah FOR THE Crossing Over

Now this is the *mitzvah*, the laws and rulings which ADONAI your God ordered me to TEACH you for you to obey in the land you are crossing over to possess, ² so that you will fear ADONAI your God and observe all his regulations and *mitzvot* that I am giving you — you, your child and your grandchild — as long as you live, and so that you will have a long life. ³ Therefore listen, Isra'el, and take care to obey, so that things will go well with you, and so that you will increase greatly, as ADONAI, the God of your ancestors, promised you by giving you a land flowing with milk and honey.

(A:vi, S: v) ⁴ *Sh'ma, Yisra'el! ADONAI Eloheinu, ADONAI echad* [Hear, Isra'el! ADONAI our God, ADONAI is one]; ⁵ and you are to Love ADONAI your God with all your heart, all your being and all your resources. ⁶ These words, which I am ordering you today, are to be on your heart; ⁷ and you are to TEACH them carefully to your children. You are to talk about them when you sit at home when you are traveling on the road, when you lie down and when you get up. ⁸ Tie them on your hand as a sign put them at the front of a headband around your forehead, ⁹ and write them on the door-frames of your house and on your gates.

(S: vi) ¹⁰ When ADONAI your God has brought you into the land he swore to your ancestors Avraham, Yitz'chak and Ya'akov that he would give you — cities great and prosperous, which you didn't build; ¹¹ houses full of all sorts of good things, which you didn't fill; water cisterns dug out, which you didn't dig; vineyards and olive trees, which you didn't plant — and you have eaten your fill; ¹² then be careful not to forget ADONAI, who brought you out of the land of Egypt, where you lived as slaves. ¹³ You are to fear ADONAI your God, serve Him and swear by his name. ¹⁴ You are not to follow other Gods, chosen from the Gods of the peoples around you; ¹⁵ because ADONAI, your God, who is here with you, is a jealous God. If you do, the anger of ADONAI your God will flare up against you and he will destroy you from the face of the Earth. ¹⁶ Do not put ADONAI your God to the test, as you tested Him at Massah [testing]. ¹⁷ Observe diligently the mitzvot of ADONAI your God, and his instructions and laws which he has given you. ¹⁸ You are to do what is right and good in the sight of ADONAI, so that things will go well with you, and you will enter and possess the good land ADONAI swore to your ancestors, ¹⁹ expelling all your enemies ahead of you, as ADONAI said.

~ Deuteronomy 6: 1-19
Complete Jewish Bible (CJB)

Time to Remove my Duality Masks

Assessing Your Direction

*Had enough of the Fruit from the Tree of KNOWledge?
Done playing with **Good and Evil**?
Are you Hungry NOW for the Fruit from the Tree of LIFE?*

*Then you must Come and pass by ANUBIS,
the Egyptian god of the dead
and protector of the Gates to the Underworld.*

You have found a Sacred Secret Path...

Ready?

SECTION ONE

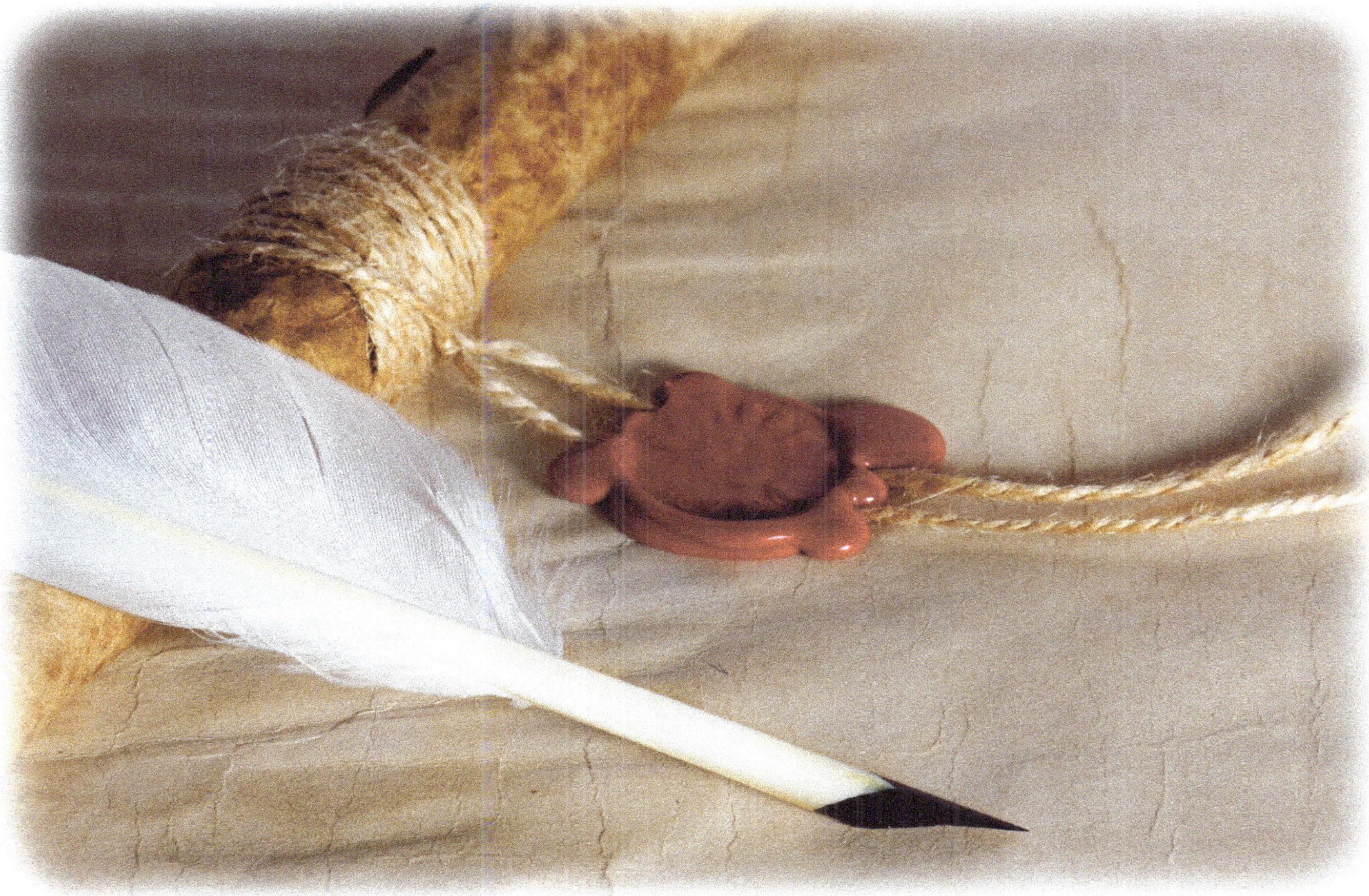

Remember...

Be patient and go deep within for your answers...

Choose the representation for the Earth School Lesson or What You Know Now:
Place your Drawing or Photo Here

Earth School Duality Lesson of *Abandonment*

Matrix Definition means the act of leaving permanently or for a long time: a place, thing, or person, especially when you should not do so. To forsake completely: desert or leave behind.

How did you FIRST experience this?

What did it TEACH you?

What do you know about **NEVER ALONE** NOW?

What promises from SACRED TEXTS did you learn?

Earth School Duality Lesson of *Betrayal*

Matrix Definition means the breaking or violation of a presumptive contract, trust, or confidence that produces moral and psychological conflict within a relationship.

How did you FIRST experience this? _____
_____
_____
_____
_____
_____
_____
_____
_____
_____

What did it TEACH you? _____
_____
_____
_____
_____
_____
_____
_____
_____
_____

What do you know about **FAITHFULNESS** NOW? _____
_____
_____
_____
_____
_____
_____
_____
_____

What promises from SACRED TEXTS did you learn? _____
_____
_____
_____
_____
_____
_____
_____
_____

Choose the representation for the
Earth School Lesson or
What You Know Now:
Place your Drawing or Photo Here

Earth School Duality Lesson of *Resentment*
Matrix Definition means a feeling of anger or displeasure about someone or something unfair.

How did you FIRST experience this? _____

What did it TEACH you? _____

What do you know about **PLEASURE** NOW? _____

What promises from SACRED TEXTS did you learn? _____

Earth School Duality Lesson of *Judgment*

Matrix Definition means the forming of an opinion, estimate, notion, or conclusion, as from circumstances presented to the mind.

How did you FIRST experience this? _____

What did it TEACH you? _____

What do you know about **FORGIVENESS** NOW? _____

What promises from SACRED TEXTS did you learn? _____

Earth School Duality Lesson of *Envy*

Matrix Definition means a longing to possess something awarded to or achieved by another.

How did you FIRST experience this? _____

What did it TEACH you? _____

What do you know about **FRIENDLINESS** NOW? _____

What promises from SACRED TEXTS did you learn? _____

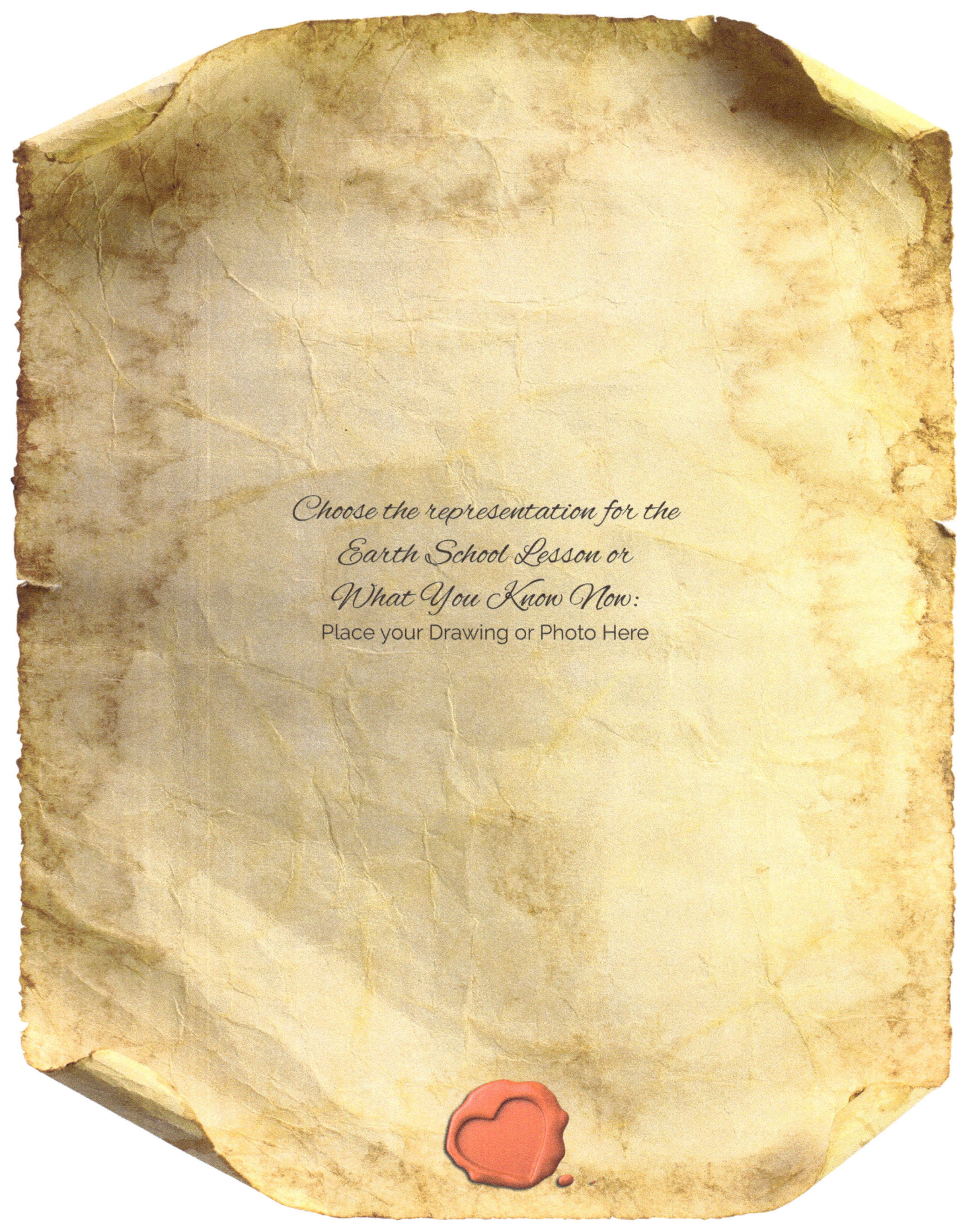

Earth School Duality Lesson of *Surprise*

Matrix Definition means feeling or showing amazement or wonder because something has happened that you did not expect or happens suddenly.

How did you FIRST experience this? _____

What did it TEACH you? _____

What do you know about **ENGAGEMENT** NOW? _____

What promises from SACRED TEXTS did you learn? _____

Choose the representation for the Earth School Lesson or What You Know Now:
Place your Drawing or Photo Here

Earth School Duality Lesson of *Cruelty*

Matrix Definition means unkind or acts, or indifference to someone's feelings or emotions, to endanger life or health or to cause mental suffering or fear, inhumane treatment; intentional or criminally negligent acts that cause pain and suffering to animals and humans.

How did you FIRST experience this? _____
_____
_____
_____
_____
_____
_____
_____
_____
_____

What did it TEACH you? _____
_____
_____
_____
_____
_____
_____
_____
_____

What do you know about **KINDNESS** NOW?_____
_____
_____
_____
_____
_____
_____
_____
_____

What promises from SACRED TEXTS did you learn? _____
_____
_____
_____
_____
_____
_____
_____
_____

Earth School Duality Lesson of *Greed*

Matrix Definition means intense and selfish desire for more of something, especially wealth, power, or food; an excessive.

How did you FIRST experience this?

What did it TEACH you?

What do you know about **GIVING** NOW?

What promises from SACRED TEXTS did you learn?

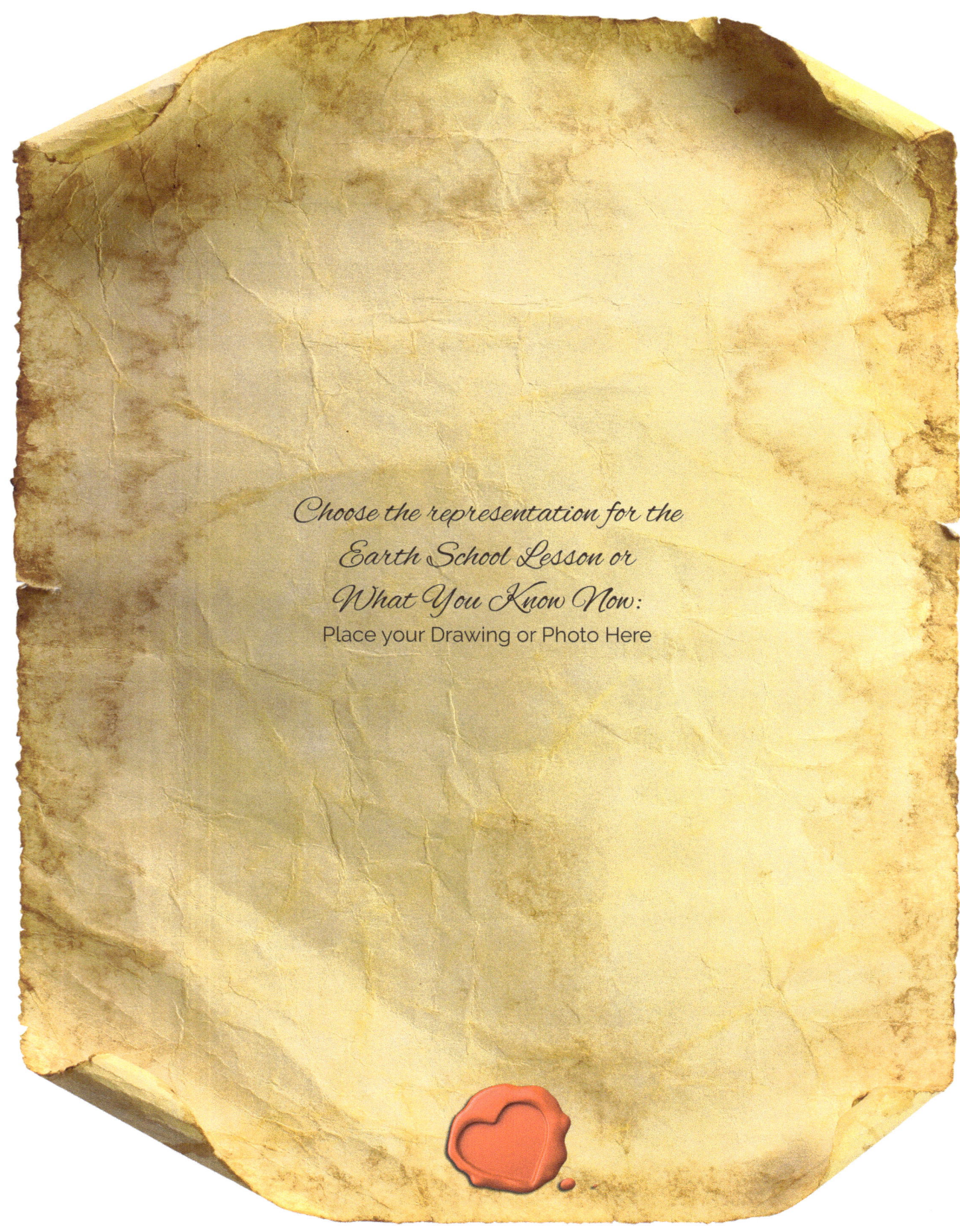

Choose the representation for the
Earth School Lesson or
What You Know Now:
Place your Drawing or Photo Here

Earth School Duality Lesson of *Grief*

Matrix Definition means deep sorrow, especially that caused by someone's Death to which a bond or affection was formed. A multifaceted natural response to loss; It is the emotional suffering one feels when something or someone the individual Loves is taken away.

How did you FIRST experience this? _____

What did it TEACH you? _____

What do you know about **JOY** NOW? _____

What promises from SACRED TEXTS did you learn? _____

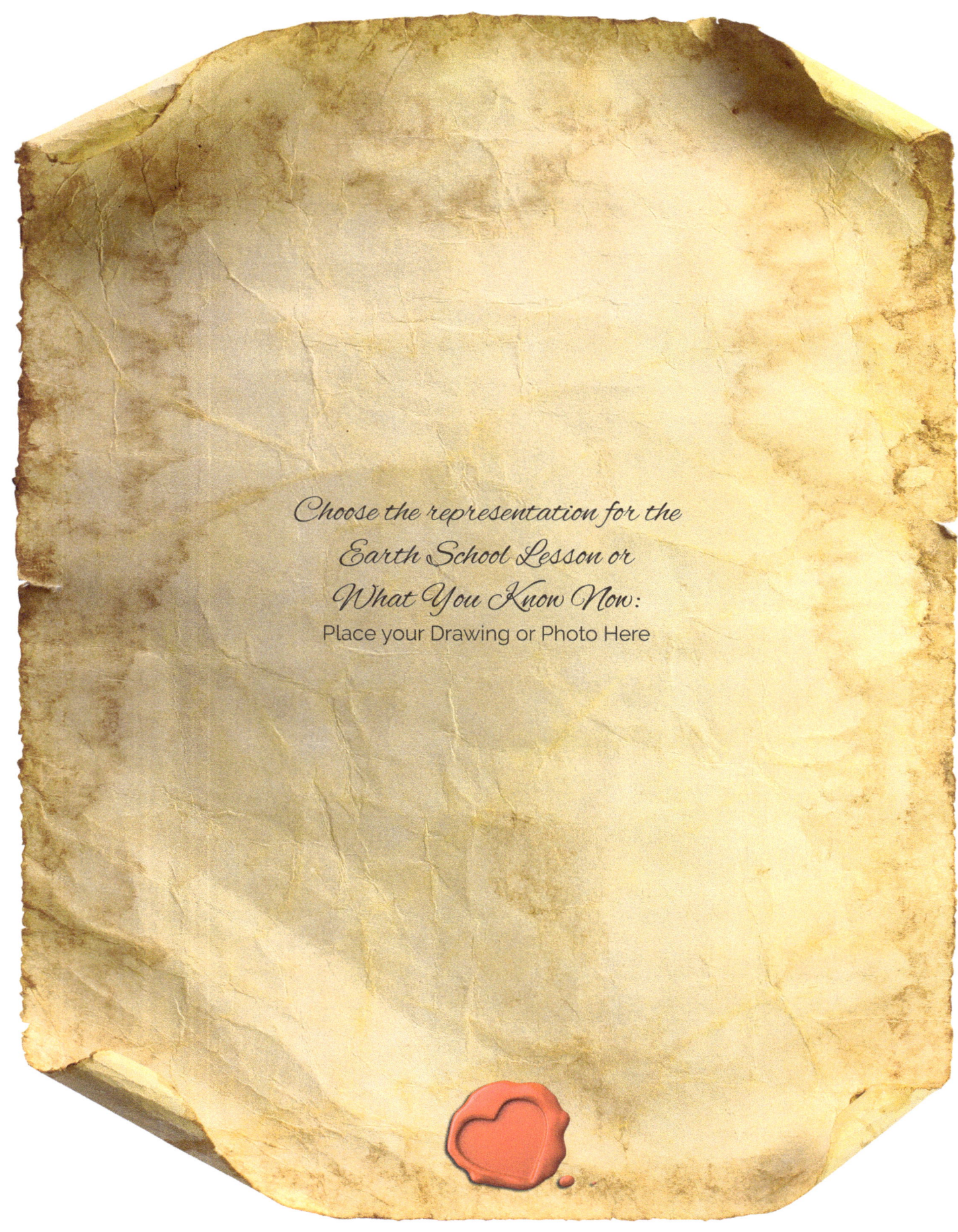

Choose the representation for the Earth School Lesson or What You Know Now:
Place your Drawing or Photo Here

Earth School Duality Lesson of *Pity*

Matrix Definition means a feeling of sadness or sympathy for someone else's unhappiness or difficult situation implying tender or sometimes slightly contemptuous sorrow for one in misery, distress, and sadness.

How did you FIRST experience this? _____

What did it TEACH you? _____

What do you know about **COMPASSION** NOW? _____

What promises from SACRED TEXTS did you learn? _____

Choose the representation for the Earth School Lesson or What You Know Now:
Place your Drawing or Photo Here

Earth School Duality Lesson of *Isolation*

Matrix Definition means to set something apart from others, completely alone, exile, hiding, quarantine, banishment. The state of being separated from other people, or a situation in which you do not have the support of other people.

How did you FIRST experience this? ___

What did it TEACH you? ___

What do you know about **PUBLIC** NOW? ___

What promises from SACRED TEXTS did you learn? ___

Choose the representation for the Earth School Lesson or What You Know Now:
Place your Drawing or Photo Here

Earth School Duality Lesson of *Shame*

Matrix Definition means a painful feeling of humiliation or distress caused by the consciousness of wrong or foolish behavior. A condition of humiliating disgrace or a state of low esteem.

How did you FIRST experience this? _____
_____
_____
_____
_____
_____
_____
_____
_____

What did it TEACH you? _____
_____
_____
_____
_____
_____
_____
_____
_____

What do you know about **CONFIDENCE** NOW? _____
_____
_____
_____
_____
_____
_____
_____
_____

What promises from SACRED TEXTS did you learn? _____
_____
_____
_____
_____
_____
_____
_____
_____

*Choose the representation for the
Earth School Lesson or
What You Know Now:*
Place your Drawing or Photo Here

Earth School Duality Lesson of *Indignation*

Matrix Definition means composed of anger, disgust, contempt, and resentment. Simply defined as anger that is caused by something that is unfair or wrong and implicitly perceived as injurious to the self-concept.

How did you FIRST experience this? _____

What did it TEACH you? _____

What do you know about **RESPECT** NOW? _____

What promises from SACRED TEXTS did you learn? _____

Let's do this!

SECTION TWO

Take your time...

Go **DEEPER** with your answers...

Choose the representation for the Earth School Lesson or What You Know Now:
Place your Drawing or Photo Here

Earth School Duality Lesson of *Sadness*

Matrix Definition means an emotional pain associated with, or characterized by, feelings of disadvantage, loss, despair, grief, helplessness, regret, disappointment, and sorrow.

How did you FIRST experience this? _____
_____
_____
_____
_____
_____
_____
_____
_____

What did it TEACH you? _____
_____
_____
_____
_____
_____
_____
_____
_____

What do you know about **HOPEFULNESS** NOW? _____
_____
_____
_____
_____
_____
_____
_____

What promises from SACRED TEXTS did you learn? _____
_____
_____
_____
_____
_____
_____
_____
_____

*Choose the representation for the
Earth School Lesson or
What You Know Now:*
Place your Drawing or Photo Here

Earth School Duality Lesson of *Enmity*

Matrix Definition means the state or feeling of being actively opposed or hostile to someone or something. A hatred such as might be felt for an enemy.

How did you FIRST experience this? _____

What did it TEACH you? _____

What do you know about **FRIENDSHIP** NOW? _____

What promises from SACRED TEXTS did you learn? _____

© Copyright 2020   Christed Bride dot com LLC | All Rights Reserved

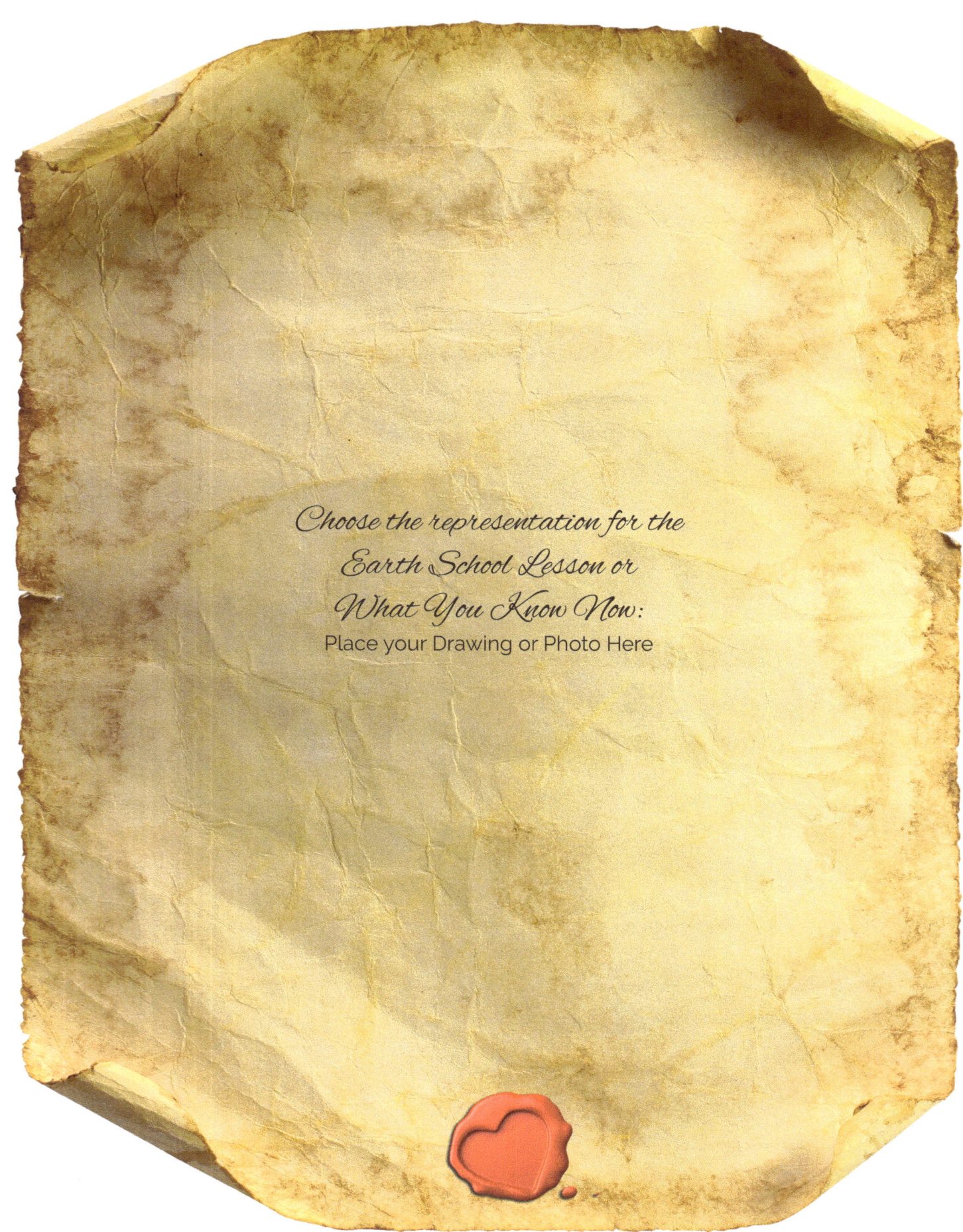

Choose the representation for the Earth School Lesson or What You Know Now:
Place your Drawing or Photo Here

Earth School Duality Lesson of *Lonely*

Matrix Definition means to be sad or unhappy because of being alone or do not have anyone to talk to during a situation or period of time.

How did you FIRST experience this? _____
_____
_____
_____
_____
_____
_____
_____

What did it TEACH you? _____
_____
_____
_____
_____
_____
_____
_____

What do you know about **LOVED** NOW? _____
_____
_____
_____
_____
_____
_____
_____

What promises from SACRED TEXTS did you learn? _____
_____
_____
_____
_____
_____
_____
_____

© Copyright 2020 | Christed Bride dot com LLC | All Rights Reserved

Choose the representation for the
Earth School Lesson or
What You Know Now:
Place your Drawing or Photo Here

Earth School Duality Lesson of *Bewitched*

Matrix Definition means to influence or affect especially injuriously by witchcraft, to cast a spell over or interest someone a lot so that you have the power to influence them.

How did you FIRST experience this? _____

What did it TEACH you? _____

What do you know about **LET GO** NOW? _____

What promises from SACRED TEXTS did you learn? _____

Choose the representation for the Earth School Lesson or What You Know Now:
Place your Drawing or Photo Here

Earth School Duality Lesson of *Defiance*

Matrix Definition means an open resistance, bold disobedience, or disregard for authority or to any opposing force, challenging attitude or behavior; open disregard, contempt.

How did you FIRST experience this?

What did it TEACH you?

What do you know about **PEACE** NOW?

What promises from SACRED TEXTS did you learn?

Choose the representation for the
Earth School Lesson or
What You Know Now:
Place your Drawing or Photo Here

Earth School Duality Lesson of *Loathing*

Matrix Definition means a strong feeling of disliking something or someone very much, to feel disgust or aversion.

How did you FIRST experience this? _____

What did it TEACH you? _____

What do you know about **APPROVAL** NOW? _____

What promises from SACRED TEXTS did you learn? _____

Choose the representation for the Earth School Lesson or What You Know Now:
Place your Drawing or Photo Here

Earth School Duality Lesson of *Rage*

Matrix Definition means to feel or express violent uncontrollable anger.

How did you FIRST experience this? _____

What did it TEACH you? _____

What do you know about **HARMONY NOW**? _____

What promises from SACRED TEXTS did you learn? _____

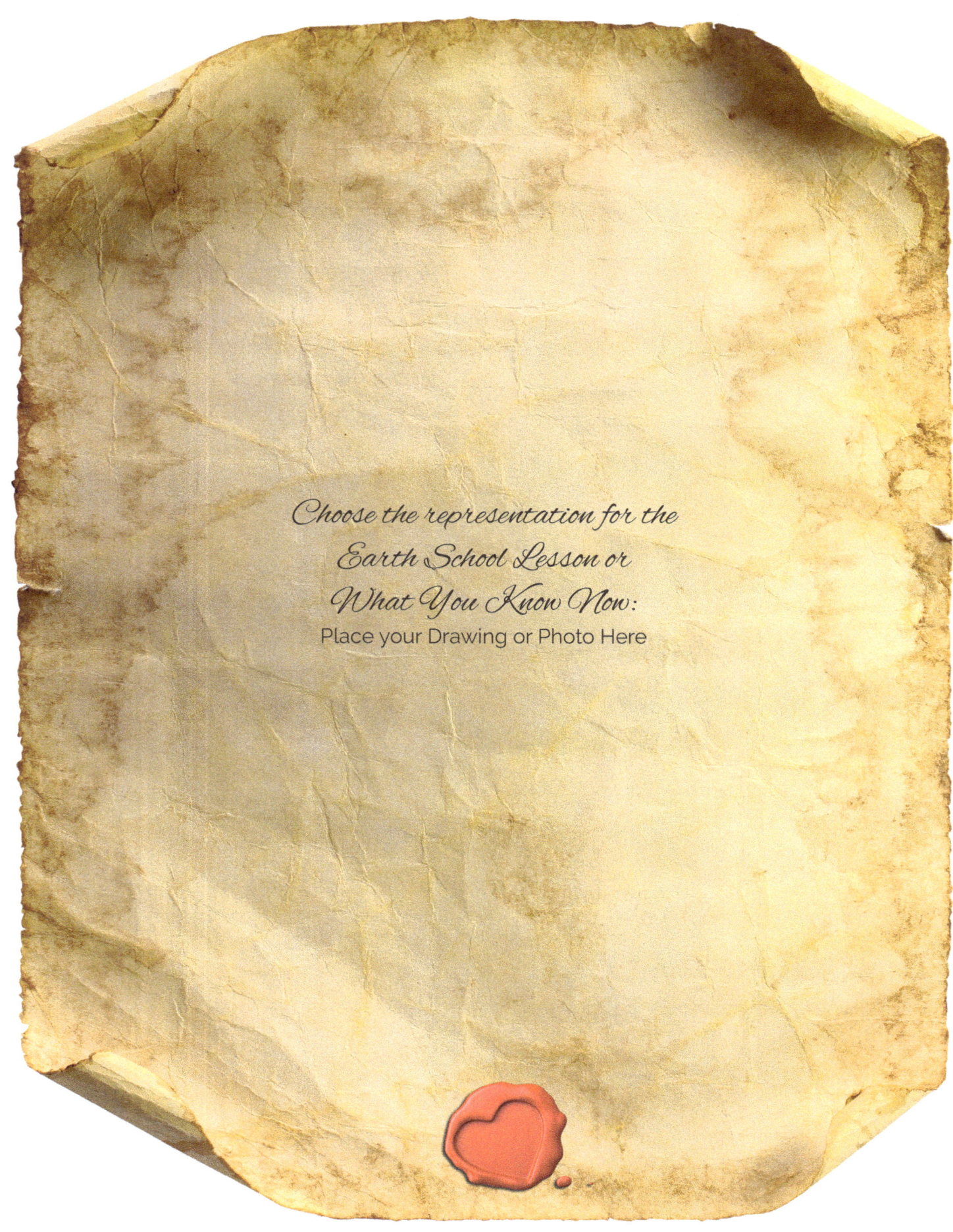

Choose the representation for the Earth School Lesson or What You Know Now:
Place your Drawing or Photo Here

Earth School Duality Lesson of *Pain*
Matrix Definition means Pain is a distressing feeling often caused by intense or damaging stimuli.

How did you FIRST experience this? _____

What did it TEACH you? _____

What do you know about **ASSISTANCE** NOW? _____

What promises from SACRED TEXTS did you learn? _____

Earth School Duality Lesson of *Vexed*

Matrix Definition means (of a problem or issue) difficult and much-debated; problematic; annoyed, frustrated, or worried.

How did you FIRST experience this? _____

What did it TEACH you? _____

What do you know about **QUIETNESS** NOW? _____

What promises from SACRED TEXTS did you learn? _____

Choose the representation for the Earth School Lesson or What You Know Now:
Place your Drawing or Photo Here

Earth School Duality Lesson of *Anger*

Matrix Definition means an intense expression of emotion. It involves a strong uncomfortable and hostile response to a perceived provocation, hurt, or threat. Anger can occur when a person feels their personal boundaries are being or are about to be violated.

How did you FIRST experience this? _____
_____
_____
_____
_____
_____
_____
_____
_____

What did it TEACH you? _____
_____
_____
_____
_____
_____
_____
_____
_____

What do you know about **GENTLENESS** NOW? _____
_____
_____
_____
_____
_____
_____
_____

What promises from SACRED TEXTS did you learn? _____
_____
_____
_____
_____
_____
_____
_____
_____

Choose the representation for the Earth School Lesson or What You Know Now:
Place your Drawing or Photo Here

Earth School Duality Lesson of *Torment*

Matrix Definition means to experience severe mental or physical suffering.

How did you FIRST experience this? _____

What did it TEACH you? _____

What do you know about **CONTENTMENT** NOW? _____

What promises from SACRED TEXTS did you learn? _____

Earth School Duality Lesson of *Hatred*

Matrix Definition means to invoke feelings of animosity, anger, or resentment, which can be directed against certain individuals, groups, entities, objects, behaviors, concepts, or ideas.

How did you FIRST experience this?

What did it TEACH you?

What do you know about **ADMIRATION** NOW?

What promises from SACRED TEXTS did you learn?

Choose the representation for the Earth School Lesson or What You Know Now:
Place your Drawing or Photo Here

Earth School Duality Lesson of *Fear*

Matrix Definition means an unpleasant emotion or thought that you have when you are frightened or worried by something dangerous, painful, or bad that is happening or might happen.

How did you FIRST experience this? _____
_____
_____
_____
_____
_____
_____
_____
_____

What did it TEACH you? _____
_____
_____
_____
_____
_____
_____
_____
_____

What do you know about **COURAGE** NOW?_____
_____
_____
_____
_____
_____
_____
_____

What promises from SACRED TEXTS did you learn? _____
_____
_____
_____
_____
_____
_____
_____
_____

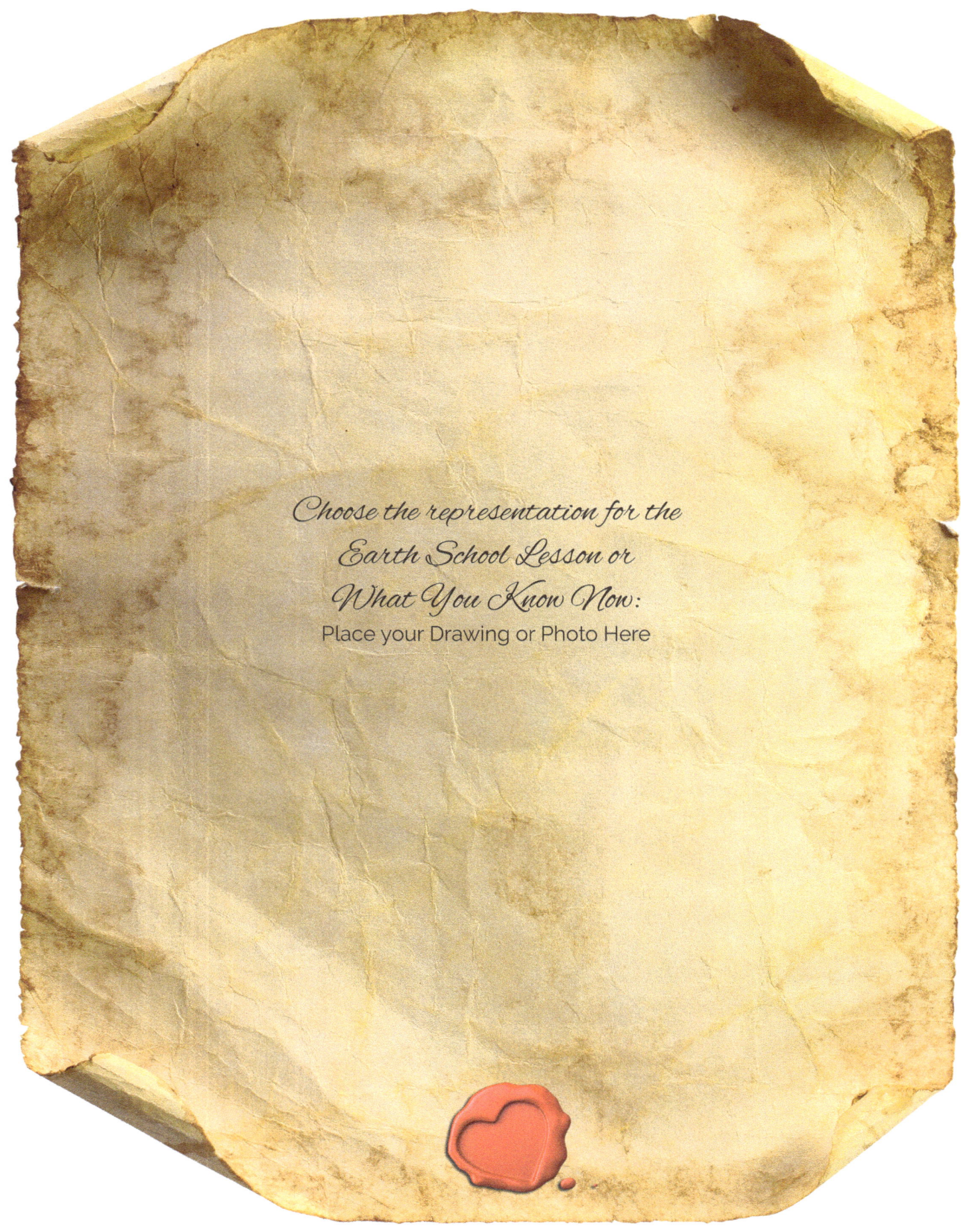

Choose the representation for the Earth School Lesson or What You Know Now:
Place your Drawing or Photo Here

Earth School Duality Lesson of *Pride*

Matrix Definition means to foolishly and irrationally corrupt one's sense of personal value, status or accomplishments or of qualities or possessions that are widely admired.

How did you FIRST experience this? _____

What did it TEACH you? _____

What do you know about **HUMILITY** NOW? _____

What promises from SACRED TEXTS did you learn? _____

Choose the representation for the Earth School Lesson or What You Know Now:
Place your Drawing or Photo Here

Earth School Duality Lesson of *Bitterness*

Matrix Definition means exhibiting strong animosity resulting from or expressive of severe grief, anguish, or disappointment and marked by resentment or cynicism.

How did you FIRST experience this? _____
_____
_____
_____
_____
_____
_____
_____
_____

What did it TEACH you? _____
_____
_____
_____
_____
_____
_____
_____
_____

What do you know about **SWEETNESS** NOW? _____
_____
_____
_____
_____
_____
_____
_____
_____

What promises from SACRED TEXTS did you learn? _____
_____
_____
_____
_____
_____
_____
_____
_____

Last Push!

SECTION THREE

*Dive into your depth for **hidden** answers...*

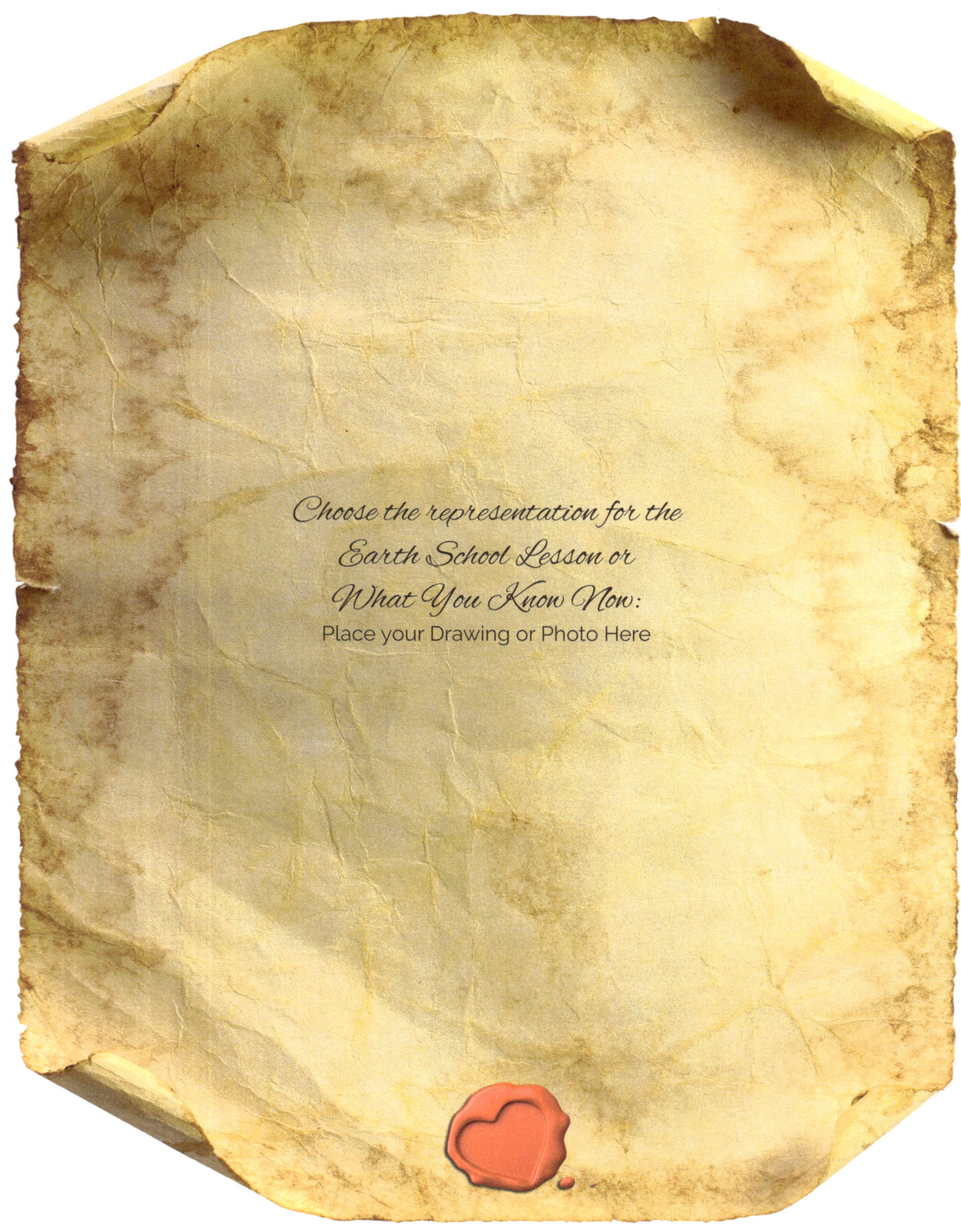

Choose the representation for the
Earth School Lesson or
What You Know Now:
Place your Drawing or Photo Here

Earth School Duality Lesson of *Lust*

Matrix Definition means a psychological force producing intense wanting for an object, or circumstance fulfilling the emotion. Lust can take any form such as the lust for sexuality, money, or power.

How did you FIRST experience this? _____

What did it TEACH you? _____

What do you know about **DIVINE LOVE** NOW? _____

What promises from SACRED TEXTS did you learn? _____

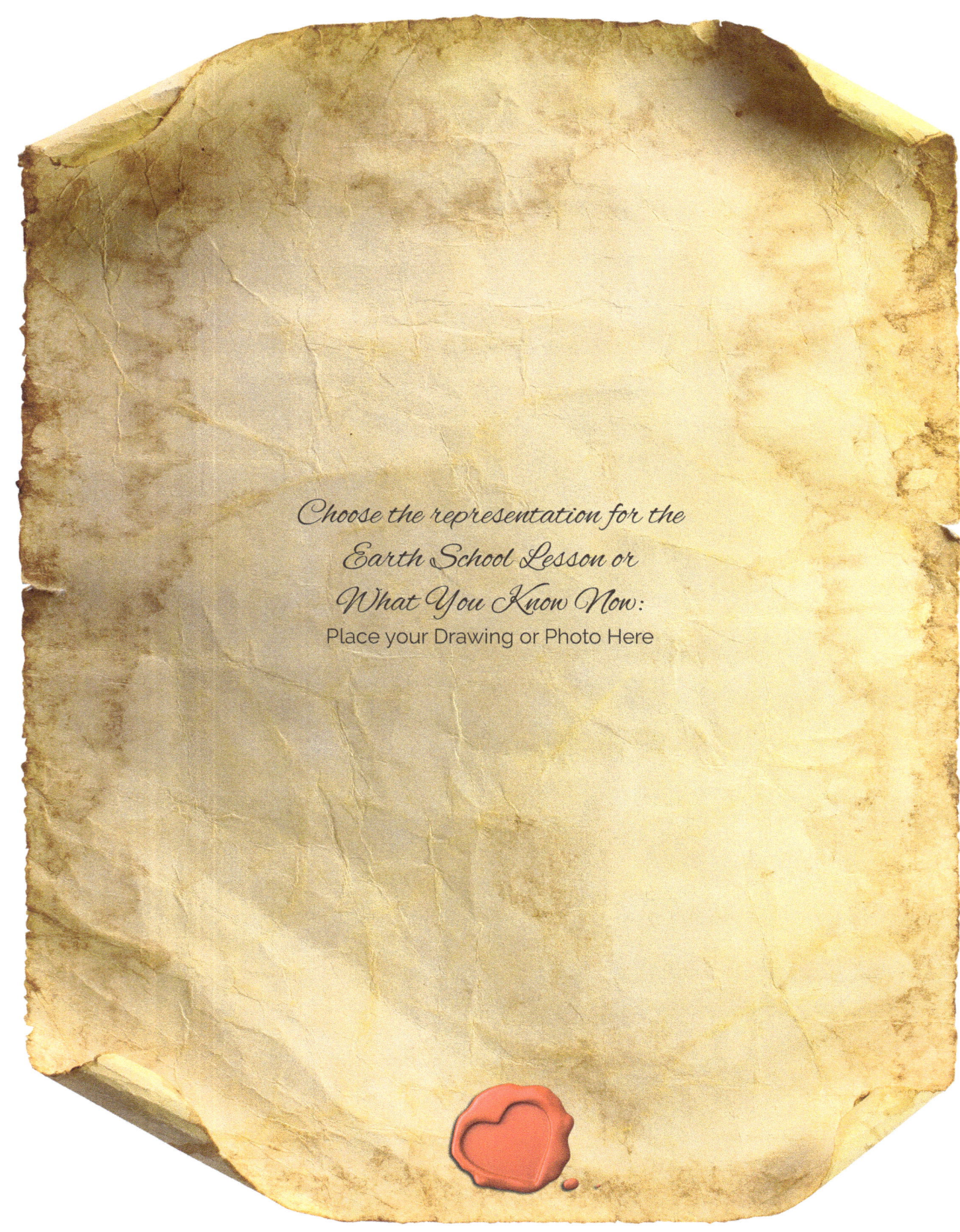

Earth School Duality Lesson of *Contempt*

Matrix Definition means a strong feeling of disliking and having no respect for someone or something. Disapproval tinged with disgust and or behavior that is illegal because it does not obey or respect the rules of law.

How did you FIRST experience this? _____

What did it TEACH you? _____

What do you know about **HONOR** NOW? _____

What promises from SACRED TEXTS did you learn? _____

Choose the representation for the Earth School Lesson or What You Know Now:
Place your Drawing or Photo Here

Earth School Duality Lesson of *Disobedience*

Matrix Definition means to deliberately not do what someone in authority tells you to do, or what a rule or law says that you should do.

How did you FIRST experience this? _____

What did it TEACH you? _____

What do you know about **SURRENDER** NOW? _____

What promises from SACRED TEXTS did you learn? _____

Choose the representation for the Earth School Lesson or What You Know Now:
Place your Drawing or Photo Here

Earth School Duality Lesson of *Disgust*

Matrix Definition means a strong feeling of disapproval and dislike at a situation or person's behavior or to something considered offensive or distasteful, or unpleasant.

How did you FIRST experience this? _____
_____
_____
_____
_____
_____
_____
_____
_____

What did it TEACH you? _____
_____
_____
_____
_____
_____
_____
_____

What do you know about **LIKING** NOW? _____
_____
_____
_____
_____
_____
_____
_____

What promises from SACRED TEXTS did you learn? _____
_____
_____
_____
_____
_____
_____
_____
_____

Choose the representation for the
Earth School Lesson or
What You Know Now:
Place your Drawing or Photo Here

Earth School Duality Lesson of *Disenchanted*

Matrix Definition means to no longer believe in the value of something, especially having learned of the problems with it. Disappointed by someone or something previously respected or admired; disillusioned.

How did you FIRST experience this? _____
_____
_____
_____
_____
_____
_____
_____
_____
_____

What did it TEACH you? _____
_____
_____
_____
_____
_____
_____
_____
_____

What do you know about **ENCOURAGED** NOW? _____
_____
_____
_____
_____
_____
_____
_____
_____

What promises from SACRED TEXTS did you learn? _____
_____
_____
_____
_____
_____
_____
_____
_____
_____

Choose the representation for the
Earth School Lesson or
What You Know Now:
Place your Drawing or Photo Here

Earth School Duality Lesson of *Separation*
Matrix Definition means the act or process of moving apart or forcing something apart.

How did you FIRST experience this? _____
_____
_____
_____
_____
_____
_____
_____
_____
_____

What did it TEACH you? _____
_____
_____
_____
_____
_____
_____
_____
_____
_____

What do you know about **UNION** NOW? _____
_____
_____
_____
_____
_____
_____
_____
_____

What promises from SACRED TEXTS did you learn? _____
_____
_____
_____
_____
_____
_____
_____
_____
_____

Choose the representation for the Earth School Lesson or What You Know Now:
Place your Drawing or Photo Here

Earth School Duality Lesson of *Doubt*

Matrix Definition means indecision between belief and disbelief. It may involve uncertainty, distrust or lack of conviction on certain facts, actions, motives, or decisions.

How did you FIRST experience this? _____

What did it TEACH you? _____

What do you know about TRUST NOW? _____

What promises from SACRED TEXTS did you learn? _____

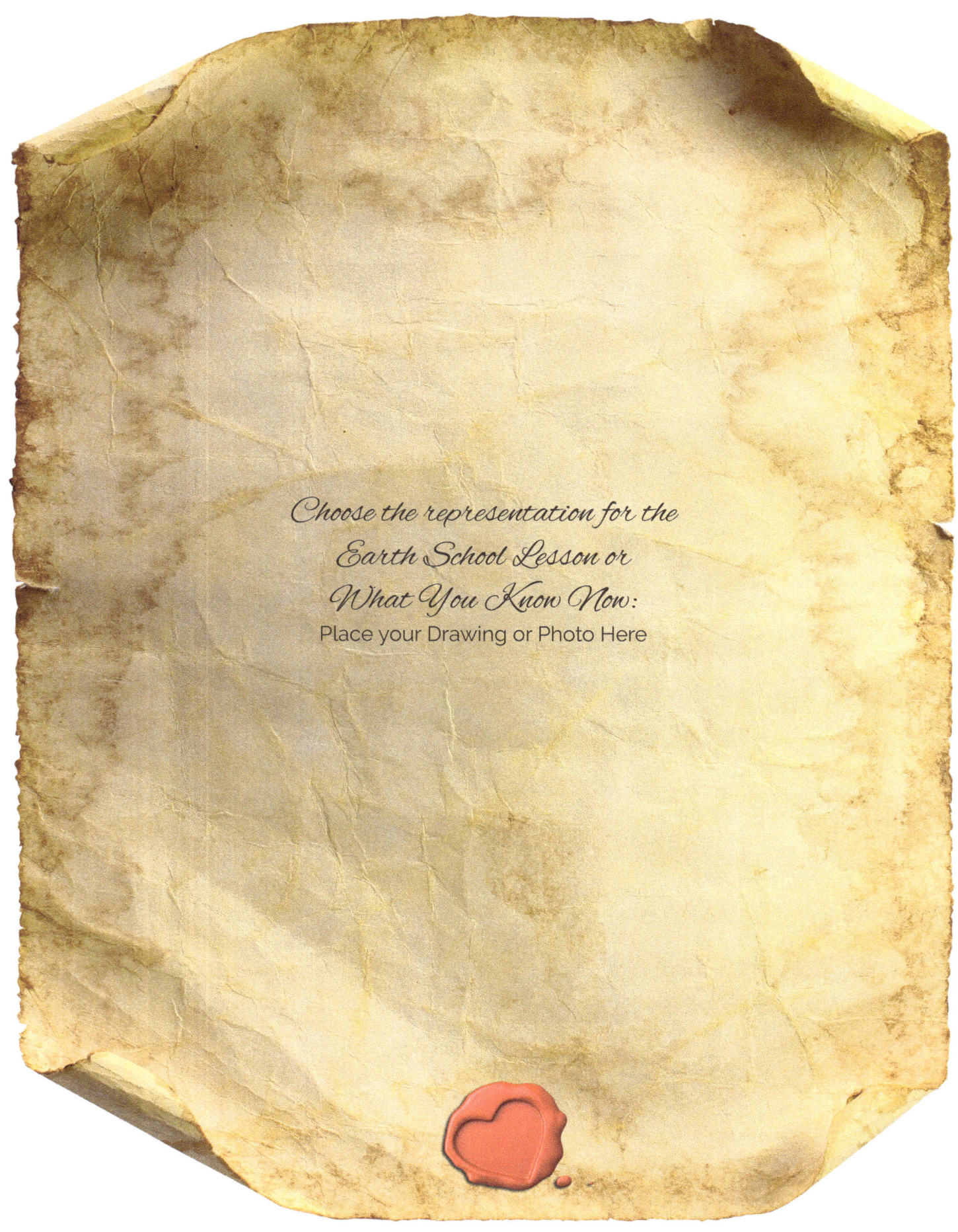

Earth School Duality Lesson of *Remorse*

Matrix Definition means a distressing emotion experienced by a person who regrets actions which they deem to be shameful, hurtful, or violent.

How did you FIRST experience this?

What did it TEACH you?

What do you know about **HAPPINESS** NOW?

What promises from SACRED TEXTS did you learn?

Choose the representation for the Earth School Lesson or What You Know Now:
Place your Drawing or Photo Here

Earth School Duality Lesson of *Disapproval*

Matrix Definition means a possession or expression of an unfavorable opinion; the feeling of having a negative opinion of someone or something, the expression or feeling that something done or said, is wrong.

How did you FIRST experience this? _____
_____
_____
_____
_____
_____
_____
_____
_____

What did it TEACH you? _____
_____
_____
_____
_____
_____
_____
_____
_____

What do you know about **ENDORSED** NOW? _____
_____
_____
_____
_____
_____
_____
_____
_____

What promises from SACRED TEXTS did you learn? _____
_____
_____
_____
_____
_____
_____
_____
_____

© Copyright 2020   Christed Bride dot com LLC | All Rights Reserved

Choose the representation for the Earth School Lesson or What You Know Now:
Place your Drawing or Photo Here

Earth School Duality Lesson of *Distrust*

Matrix Definition means to doubt the honesty or reliability of; regard with suspicion; a formal way of not trusting any one party too much in a situation of grave risk or deep doubt. "Trust, but verify".

How did you FIRST experience this? _____

What did it TEACH you? _____

What do you know about **OPTIMISM** NOW? _____

What promises from SACRED TEXTS did you learn? _____

Choose the representation for the Earth School Lesson or What You Know Now:

Place your Drawing or Photo Here

Earth School Duality Lesson of *Dispair*
Matrix Definition means the complete loss or absence of hope.

How did you FIRST experience this? _____

What did it TEACH you? _____

What do you know about **HOPE** NOW? _____

What promises from SACRED TEXTS did you learn? _____

Earth School Duality Lesson of *Guilt*

Matrix Definition means when a person believes or realizes—accurately or not—that they have compromised their own standards of conduct or have violated a universal moral standard and bear significant responsibility for that violation.

How did you FIRST experience this? _____
_____
_____
_____
_____
_____
_____
_____
_____
_____

What did it TEACH you? _____
_____
_____
_____
_____
_____
_____
_____
_____

What do you know about CLEANSED NOW? _____
_____
_____
_____
_____
_____
_____
_____

What promises from SACRED TEXTS did you learn? _____
_____
_____
_____
_____
_____
_____
_____
_____

THE Pivotal Question

— TIME NOW FOR YOU TO MAKE —

one of two choices:

Either

Die and leave Your Earth-Suit behind

Or

Die out to Self...
"Surrender your Ego"...
and Invoke Your Divine Birthright...
By participating in Resurrecting Your Body
back to

Your Full Glory Light...

NOW

Do you actually believe that Yahushua (Jesus) conquered Death, Hell and the Grave?

SELAH!! *(stop and think about it)*

THE Awakening

Inscribed on the altar at a temple of the Goddess Isis in Egypt are the following words:

"I am she who separated Heaven from the Earth.
I have instructed mankind in the mysteries.
I have pointed out their paths to the stars.
I have ordered the course of the Sun and the Moon.
I am Queen of the rivers and winds and sea.
I have brought together men and women.
I gave mankind their laws, and ordained what no one can alter.
I have made justice more powerful than silver and gold.
I have caused truth to be considered beautiful.
I am she who is called the Goddess of Women.
I, Isis am all that has been, that is or shall be.
No mortal man hath ever me unveiled.
The fruit which I have brought forth is the Sun."

Hear me, Sons of Light, for I will impart to you the gift of tongues, that by speaking to your Earthly Mother in the morning, and to your Heavenly Father in the evening, you may go closer and closer to oneness with the kingdoms of Earth and Heaven, that oneness for which the Son of Man is destined from the beginning of the times.

~ *Excerpt from: Essene Gospel of Peace*

— CO-CREATING HEAVEN ON EARTH —

Begins With You

Through Divine Union...

**Your Earth-Suit... Sanctified
In perfect Union
with
Your Holy Spirit**

*Yahushua (Jesus) taught us how to work with the
Angels in the Essene Scriptures
as quoted from the
Gospel of Peace, Book 1-4*

https://reluctant-messenger.com/essene/gospel_of_peace.htm

...As the Universe, So the Soul...

~ by Hermes Trismegistus

And Yahushua (Jesus) spoke:

As the Son inherits the land of his Father, so have we inherited a Holy Land from our Fathers.

This land is not a field to be plowed, but a place within us where we may build our Holy Temple. And even as a temple must be raised, stone by stone, so will I give to you those stones for the building of the Holy Temple; that which we have inherited from our Fathers, and their Fathers' Fathers.

And all the men gathered around Yahushua (Jesus), and their faces shone with desire to hear the words which would come from his lips. And he lifted his face to the rising sun, and the radiance of its rays filled his evyes as he spoke:

The Holy Temple can be built only with the ancient Communions,

Those which are spoken, those which are thought, and those which are lived.

For if they are spoken only with the mouth, they are as a dead hive which the bees have forsaken, that gives no more honey.

The Communions are a bridge between man and the Angels, and like a bridge, can be built only with patience, yea, even as the bridge over the river is fashioned stone by stone, as they are found by the water's edge.

And the Communions are fourteen in number, as the Angels of the Heavenly Father number seven,

And the Angels of the Earthly Mother number seven.

And just as the roots of the tree sink into the Earth and are nourished, and the branches of the tree Raise their arms to Heaven,

So is man like the trunk of the tree,

with his roots deep in the breast of his Earthly Mother,

And his soul ascending to the bright stars of his Heavenly Father

And the roots of the tree are the Angels of the Earthly Mother,

And the branches of the tree are the Angels of the Heavenly Father.

And this is the Sacred Tree of Life which stands in the Sea of Eternity.

~ Excerpts from: The Essene Gospel of Peace, Book Two

The Decision

TRANS-MORPHO-GENETICS

Parting the Veils of Illusion

THE 7 Hermetic Principles

"The Principle of Truth are Seven; he who knows these, understandingly, posses the Magic Key before whose touch, all the Doors of the Temple fly open."

~ The Kybalion

1. The Principle of Mentalism
The All is Mind; the Universe is Mental.

2. The Principle of Correspondence
As Above, so Below, As Below, so Above.

3. The Principle of Vibration
Nothing Rests, Everything Moves; Everything Vibrates.

4. The Principle of Polarity
Everything is Dual; Everything has Poles; Everything has its Pair of Opposites.

5. The Principle of Rhythm
The Pendulum swing Manifests in everything; the Measure of the Swaying to the Right is a Measure of the Swaying to the Left; Rhythm Compensates.

6. The Principle of Cause and Effect
Every Cause has Effect; Every Effect has its Cause.

7. The Principle of Gender is in Everything;
Everything has its Masculine and Feminine Principles; Gender Manifests on all Planes.

QUOTED: Hermes Trismegistus

Now, I am Ready...
to
Lay Down my Life
As a Living Sacrifice

~ Romans 12:1 Complete Jewish Bible (CJB)

I exhort you, therefore, brothers, in view of God's mercies,
to offer yourselves as a sacrifice,
living and set apart for God. This will please him;
it is the logical "Temple worship" for you.

Ascension

The Invitation

¹⁶ "I, Yahushua, have sent my Angel to give you this testimony for the Messianic communities. I am the Root and Offspring of David, the bright Morning Star.

¹⁷ The Spirit and the Bride say, 'Come!'
Let anyone who hears say, 'Come!'
And let anyone who is thirsty come — let anyone who wishes, take the water of life free of charge."

~ Revelation 22:16-17
Complete Jewish Bible (CJB)

Glorified Body Restoring

Cocooned

I am Grateful, Heavenly Father, for
Thou hast Raised me to an
Eternal Height and I walk in the
Wonders of the Plain.

Thou gavest me Guidance to reach
Thine Eternal Company from the
Depths of the Earth.
Thou hast Purified my Body to join the
Army of the Angels of the Earth and my
Spirit to reach the Congregation of the Heavenly Angels.

Thou gavest Man Eternity to
Praise at Dawn and Dusk
Thy Works and Wonders in Joyful Song.

~ from the Thanksgiving Psalms, of the Dead Sea Scrolls

A Cocooned Image:
Place your Drawing or Photo Here

Born Again

I have reached the Inner Vision
and through
Thy Spirit in me
I have heard Thy Wondrous Secret.

Through Thy Mystic Insight
Thou hast caused a Spring of Knowledge
to Well Up within Me,
a Fountain of Power,
Pouring forth Living Waters,

a Flood of Love
and
of All-Embracing Wisdom
like the
Splendor of Eternal Light.

~ from the Book of Hymns of the Dead Sea Scrolls

A New Birth or Born Again Image:
Place your Drawing or Photo Here

THE FOUNTAIN OF
Living Waters

*I Thank Thee, Heavenly Father, because
Thou hast put Me at a
Source of Running Streams,
at a Living Spring in a Land of Drought,*

*Watering an Eternal Garden of Wonders,
the Tree of Life,
Mystery of Mysteries,*

*Growing everlasting Branches for
Eternal Planting to sink their Roots
into the Stream of Life from
an Eternal Source.*

*And Thou, Heavenly Father,
Protect their Fruits with the
Angels of the Day and of the Night
and with Flames of Eternal Light*

Burning every Way.

~ from the Thanksgiving Psalm, of the Dead Sea Scrolls

A Living Water Image:
(pouring life through and out to others)
Place your Drawing or Photo Here

— TIME TO TURN "OUR" LIGHTS ON FROM THE INSIDE OUT AND —

Get this Party Started!

1 Corinthians 15:52-54
Complete Jewish Bible (CJB)

It will take but a moment, the blink of an eye, at the final Shofar. For the Shofar will sound, and the dead will be raised to live Forever, and we too will be changed. For this material which can decay must be clothed with imperishability, this which is mortal must be clothed with immortality. When what decays puts on imperishability and what is mortal puts on immortality, then this passage in the Tanakh will be fulfilled:

"Death is swallowed up in Victory."

Forever Yours,

"SonShine Rose"
Yahushua's Christed Bride

To Order

COLLECTOR'S EDITION
Resurrection Journey of the Christed Bride
with Behind The Scenes / 10 Years in the Making

STORY
Resurrection Journey of the Christed Bride

WORKBOOK
My Resurrection Journey Invitation

WORKBOOK ONLINE WORKSHOP
40 Days of Transmutation ~ 40 Episodes

MINI BOOK
Angel Communion ~ Daily Devotional

AUDIO~VISUAL BOOK
Available in Multiple Formats

AUDIO BOOK
Available in MP3

Visit

www.ChristedBride.com

Audio  Visual

Book Preview
Resurrection Journey of the Christed Bride

Order in Various Formats
www.ChristedBride.com

Music and Voice Over Credits

BACKGROUND PIANO MUSIC "MY BELOVED"
Written and Performed by: Mario Torrez (Son)

Music Album: **KEYS TO THE KINGDOM**
By: Roz Griffin and Marieke Bos
http://mariekebos.co.za

Voice Over

God Spoken By: Glenn Mire

SonShine Rose Spoken By: *Herself*

For Further Personal Studies

THE GNOSIS ARCHIVE
www.gnosis.org

ESSENE GOSPEL OF PEACE
https://reluctant-messenger.com
www.earlychristianwritings.com
https://essene.com

THE ACADEMY FOR FUTURE SCIENCE
J.J. Hurtak, Ph.D.
www.affsusa.org
&
www.keysofenoch.org
Book and Music Catalog

— THE FOLLLOWING PAGES —

are

2 Worksheets

for

Your

Deeper

Inner

Work

— **FOR DEEP TRAUMA WORK** —

*The Template on the page
has been provided for your convenience*

Please cut out this Template Page to make copies
(see other side)

Use ❶ Sheet per Trauma

Resurrection Journey of The Christed Bride

Dare to Dream Eternal Life Here and Now • www.christedbride.com

*(Please copy this **Trauma Worksheet** for each Individual Trauma Reconciliation)*

Describe the Trauma you experienced:	List the names of Emotions you experienced:	What is the Story you told yourself for this to be true?:	What did you Learn?:	How do you use your Wisdom in your Life?:
Age:				

FOR SHIFTING BELIEFS & JUDGMENTS TO ZERO (NEUTRAL) POINT

The Template on the following page has been provided for your convenience

Please cut out this Template Page to make copies
(see other side)

Use ❶ Line for per Belief or Judgment

Examples of Shifting

BELIEF: My mother never loved me in my childhood.

SHIFTED TO: My mother didn't love herself so she could not show me the love I needed or wanted.

JUDGMENT: I hated my mother because she was a mean and very critical woman.

SHIFTED TO: My mother was not fully open yet to the Love of Mother and Father God, therefore I Bless her.

Resurrection Journey of The Christed Bride

Dare to Dream Eternal Life Here and Now • www.christedbride.com

(Please copy this Shifting Beliefs & Judgments to Zero (Neutral) Point Worksheet, if needed)

Redefine each Belief or Judgment to a Higher Vibration filled with Love, or Loving Description:

List Misaligned Beliefs you have and/or Judgments of a Person, Place, Thing or of Yourself:

CIRCLE ONE
J=Judgment
B=Belief

Photography Credits

The Bride *By istockphoto.com/NazariyKarkhut* .... Front Cover

Veiled *By John McVeety Photographer* .... Intro

Fire Burning Heart *By istockphoto.com/Adelevin* 2

Rainbow Body *By John McVeety Photographer* 3

Open Heart Leo *By Dianna Rae Adventures Photography* 9

Angel of Independence *By istockphoto.com/MBurnham* 12

Ornamental Lace *By magenta10/bigstock.com* 13

Red Drape Venetian Mask *By Dankalilly/bigstock.com* 15

Multiple Mardi Gras Masks *By jaflippo/bigstock.com* 20

Circus Tent with Scroll *By istockphoto.com/AlonzoDesign* 21

Theater Concept *By gar984/bigstock.com* 24

Greeting Anubis *By Dianna Rae Adventures Photography* 26

Watching 1 *By John McVeety Photographer* 27

Ancient Parchment Scroll *By istockphoto.com/yvdavyd* 28, 56, 88

Watching 2 *By John McVeety Photographer* 55

Watching 3 *By John McVeety Photographer* 87

Celebration *By John McVeety Photographer* 113

Twig and Heart Card *By Yakovenko Nataliia/bigstock.com* 114

Peacock *By John McVeety Photographer* 121

Beautiful Landscape *By istockphoto.com/Preto_perola* 123

Eclipsing Light-Dark *By Laser Todd Photographer* 125

Trans-morpho-genetics *By John McVeety Photographer* 128

Parting the Veils *By John McVeety Photographer* 129

Heart Petals *By istockphoto.com/Riorita* 132

Spirit & Bride *By Bonnie Atwood Photographer* 136

Love Smiles *By John McVeety Photographer* 146

White Stallion *By istockphoto.com/66North* 147

The MarieLucinda *By Dianna Rae Adventures Photography* .... Back Cover

Other Images Used

Gold Borders: Ornamental Lace By magenta10/bigstock.com
Veiled Border: Bright Colorful Rainbow By Mr.Background/bigstock.com
Christed Bride Logo Created By Artistic Designer, Kath ONeil
Dedication page: Rainbow Art By cgdeaw/bigstock.com
Romantic Scattered Hearts By artist_M/bigstock.com
Frame Isolated Black Hearts Border By Yakovenko Nataliia/bigstock.com
The Light Created By Artistic Designer, Kath ONeil
Stop Sign Border Created By Artistic Designer, Kath ONeil
Old Stained Paper By istockphoto.com/Avalon Studio
Wax Heart Seal By istockphoto.com/phive2015
Twig and Heart Card By Yakovenko Nataliia/bigstock.com
Valentine Hearts Wreath By istockphoto.com/Kaisorn
Isis Border: Imitation Stained Glass By Zagory/bigstock.com
As Above So Below Created By Artistic Designer, Kath ONeil
Trauma Worksheet Created By SonShine Rose
Shifting Beliefs and Judgments Worksheet Created By SonShine Rose
Banner of Peace Symbol http://pt.agni-yoga.com/sign_of_peace.php
Symbol of the Three Jewels (Chintamani)
  By Christopher J. Fynn/ Wikimedia Commons
  (http://commons.wikimedia.org/wiki/User:Cfynn)
  Copy of license for usage:
   http://creativecommons.org/licenses/by-sa/3.0/deed.en
  Image location:
   https://en.wikipedia.org/wiki/Refuge_(Buddhism)#/media/File:Three_Jewels_symbol_c olour.svg

Special Thanks to

Kath ONeil • oneilgallery.com • Portland, Oregon
Artistic Designer - Photo Editor - Stylist - Art Director

Model Credits

All Female Models

are

MarieLucinda Anderson "SonShine Rose"

herself.

Model photos were taken between 2006 to 2014

— PLEASE MEET THE AUTHOR —
MarieLucinda Anderson

"SonShineRose"

Even before my Birth, I was assigned as a Missionary from Heaven, for the End Time Gathering of His Children born from Above. I was filled with the Holy Ghost in my mother's womb, then lifted-up to God on the day of my Birth. I have been gifted many skills for this End Time Harvest; one is that I have spoken in Tongues (Ancient Heavenly Language) since I was 2 years old. During my childhood, my family unit was broken through Divorce. But ultimately, I was raised in Heavenly Places by Father God, Yahushua (Jesus Christ) my Master Teacher and the 38 Angels that were assigned to me here in Earth School.

My Dedication Ceremony as a pure Bride was on my 10th Birthday; July 2, 1975. During the year of 1983; I was 18 years old and on my way to work one morning - this would have been the second time Father God had spoken directly to me "Audibly". Father God called me "*SonShineRose*". I was looking around to who was saying this and then He said it again - and I recognized it was Him talking to me out loud. Then I asked... "What does that mean?" And He answered me audibly; "You are my Rose I am growing that my Son Shines through". And tears rolled down my face I was so amazed. It was such a special loving name He could call me. And on my 20th Birthday July 2, 1985, I Dedicated myself as His Disciple.

Yahushua proposed to me in June of 2010; I accepted this proposal and married Yahushua in Jewish Ceremony on my 25th Discipleship Anniversary ~ July 2, 2010. My two adult children stood in as witnesses and signed my Ketubah (Jewish marriage certificate).

I was given the Keys to the Kingdom and now can Enter into Heavenly Realms at will. I have given my Life as a Student to Yahushua. I have laid down my Life and Died out to my flesh. On October 28, 2010, I was Raised-up in Resurrection Power and continue to Transform from Glory to Glory, Every Day.

I have recorded My Resurrection Journey of the Christed Bride, so that You can learn and understand this process and apply it to your own Life Passage. The main story will take you through the many Alchemy levels of enlightenment I have experienced and the glorious outcomes I have enjoyed. I share this intimate Journey with You, breaking down the many lessons, difficult understandings and acceptances, and the final prosperity that I achieved - as a guide to help you through your own Crossing. The Workbook was created as a healing support tool for your convenience ~ so that you may dive deeply into the places holding you back from total freedom and success. May this trek elevate you and lift you to Everlasting Love and Peace and eventually back Home to the Stars.

Please visit my website: **www.ChristedBride.com** where I share with you several different tools for your Earth School Journey that have assisted me and my Temple over the years.

I am so thankful I have arrived Here and I am privileged to have met You through this vehicle of connection here in Earth School.

Many Blessings
in Your Transmutation Journey and Your Trans-Morpho-Genetic Decision.

With Great Endearments for YOU...
~ MarieLucinda Anderson

Notes

www.ingramcontent.com/pod-product-compliance
Lightning Source LLC
Chambersburg PA
CBHW042024100526
44587CB00029B/4291